EXPLORING
WONDERS OF THE WORLD

Written by
David Seidman

Incorporated

THE WONDERS BEGIN

You may think they can't be real. They're too big, beautiful, or simply amazing. They're the world's wonders, from ancient tombs to modern skyscrapers. The first wonders ever to be described are known as the *Seven Wonders of the World*. Only one of these is still in existence. But people have continued to create, and the world today is full of exciting buildings, bridges, and other awe-inspiring structures.

GREAT SURVIVOR

The three pyramids of Giza, in Egypt, are the oldest of the original seven wonders, and they're still standing. Starting 45 centuries ago, thousands of workers labored for more than 20 years. The Great Pyramid is almost 500 feet high, more than 750 feet long on each side, and weighs more than 4 million tons.

MYSTERIOUS DISAPPEARANCE

It was gold and ivory, and at least 30 feet high. Visitors worshipped at its feet. The statue of Zeus in Olympia, Greece, sat enthroned in its own temple. During the ancient Olympic Games it was a tourist attraction. The statue lasted nearly 900 years, then vanished for no apparent reason.

ART AND ARTEMIS

With marble columns 60 feet high—127 of them—Greece's temple of Artemis projected raw strength. One of Greece's largest temples, this ancient wonder stood from 550 B.C. until A.D. 262, when invaders destroyed it.

6

LET THERE BE LIGHT

The lighthouse on the island of Pharos near Alexandria, Egypt, became so famous that in many languages, *pharos* meant lighthouse. At about 400 feet high, with a flame visible for miles, the lighthouse stood for at least 1,500 years. Around the year 1300, an earthquake toppled the tower.

DYING TO BE FAMOUS

How do you become a word? Ask the Turkish king Mausolus. More than 2,300 years ago, he began to build a giant tomb for himself in Halicarnassus, his capital city. The tomb, made of gleaming white marble, became so famous that even today a big tomb is called a *mausoleum*.

THERE'S NO PLACE LIKE HOME

About 2,500 years ago, the queen of Babylon felt homesick for the hilly forests where she had lived as a girl. To cheer her up, the king built a 300-foot pyramid overflowing with plants. Centuries later, the Hanging Gardens of Babylon vanished. Today, no one knows where they once stood.

7

A BIG DEAL

The Greeks had a strong army. But when they attacked Rhodes, a small island, the islanders won. Crediting the miracle to the god Helios, the islanders built a statue for him. More than 100 feet high, the Colossus seemed indestructible. Less than a century later, though, an earthquake shattered it.

LIVING IN LUXURY

So what's it like to live like a king? It's a life of wonder. All over the world, leaders and other dignitaries have built unbelievably big and beautiful palaces and castles.

MAD LUDWIG

Atop a rock ledge in the Bavarian Alps stands a reconstruction of a medieval castle, known as Neuschwanstein. Constructed in 1869 by order of Bavaria's King Louis II, also called "Mad Ludwig," the castle contains a two-story throne room, with a ceiling decorated like a starry night sky.

▲ MYSTERY MANSION

To heiress Sarah Winchester, her palatial house did not feel like a home. Winchester rifles killed thousands, and she felt the ghosts of the fallen haunting her. To gain peace from them, she tried to trick the ghosts by having additions made to her house—stairs leading nowhere, doors opening onto walls, and hundreds of rooms.

▼ ROYAL RESIDENCE

Can you guess who makes this luxurious palace her home? Her Highness, the Queen of England. Buckingham Palace is full of treasures, but one of the most popular spectacles takes place outside—the Changing of the Guard is more for pomp and circumstance than to relieve the guards of their shift.

8

▼ FORT FANTASTIC

To build a new capital, Indian king Shah Jahan (builder of the Taj Mahal) thought big. Covering more than 5 million square feet, with walls 60 feet high, his Red Fort held not just offices and military barracks but also palaces, gardens, and fountains. Carved into one building are words meaning, "If there is a paradise on Earth, this is it."

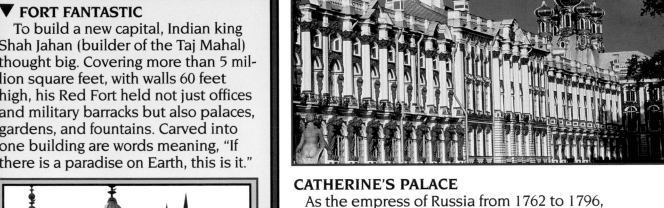

CATHERINE'S PALACE

As the empress of Russia from 1762 to 1796, Catherine the Great found that she needed a little rest from the pressures of her regal life. But her idea of a quiet country home would seem extravagant to others. As it stands today, 22 of the original rooms have been restored and the building stretches 900 feet.

SHOGUN PALACE

Atop a 150-foot-high bluff in Himeji, Japan, sits the "White Egret," the most magnificent of the 12 surviving Japanese castles. Built for military defense, the castle features openings through which defenders could pour boiling water or oil on attackers.

A COUNTRY HOME

Starting in 1661, King Louis XIV of France took a hunting lodge in the town of Versailles and turned it into the seat of government. Taking nearly 100 years to finish, the new palace and its grounds housed thousands. Its gardens included canals, pools, sculptures, and over 1,000 fountains.

The Hall of Mirrors in the palace of Versailles.

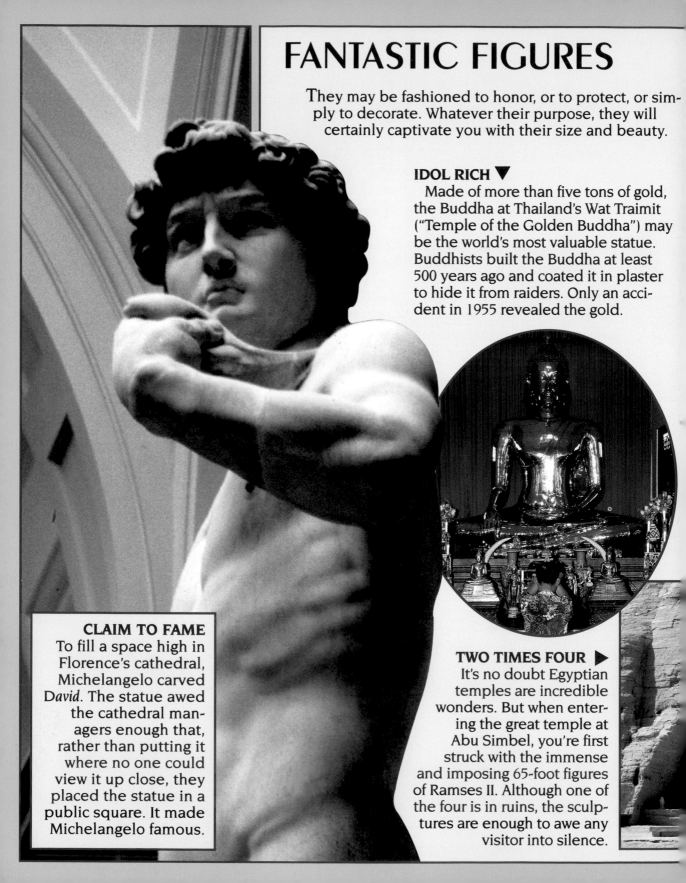

FANTASTIC FIGURES

They may be fashioned to honor, or to protect, or simply to decorate. Whatever their purpose, they will certainly captivate you with their size and beauty.

IDOL RICH ▼

Made of more than five tons of gold, the Buddha at Thailand's Wat Traimit ("Temple of the Golden Buddha") may be the world's most valuable statue. Buddhists built the Buddha at least 500 years ago and coated it in plaster to hide it from raiders. Only an accident in 1955 revealed the gold.

CLAIM TO FAME

To fill a space high in Florence's cathedral, Michelangelo carved *David*. The statue awed the cathedral managers enough that, rather than putting it where no one could view it up close, they placed the statue in a public square. It made Michelangelo famous.

TWO TIMES FOUR ▶

It's no doubt Egyptian temples are incredible wonders. But when entering the great temple at Abu Simbel, you're first struck with the immense and imposing 65-foot figures of Ramses II. Although one of the four is in ruins, the sculptures are enough to awe any visitor into silence.

TALL, TALL TOTEMS

A totem is a kind of symbol—an animal or plant—that ties a group of people together. Many peoples have totems in their society, such as Native Americans and the Aborigines of Australia. Figures of the totem are often carved from whole trees.

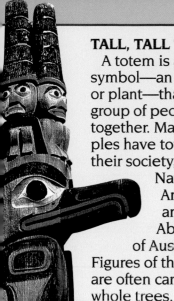

MOUNTAIN MAN

On Stone Mountain near Atlanta, Georgia, stands the world's largest sculpture— 90-foot images of Civil War leaders Robert E. Lee, Stonewall Jackson, and Jefferson Davis. Begun by Gutzon Borglum, the sculpture took more than eight years to finish. It took the same sculptor 14 years to carve Mt. Rushmore. (See end pages.)

CLAY ARMY

Do you think sculpting a life-size statue of a man would take a lot of time? More than 2,000 years ago, China's Emperor Qin demanded sculptures of over 7,000 different men, plus chariots and horses. Qin's artists carved for 36 years. When he died, his clay army was buried with him to protect him in the afterlife.

LADY FREEDOM

Alexandre Eiffel didn't work small. The Eiffel Tower's designer also built the Statue of Liberty. More than 300 feet high and weighing over 200 tons, America's tallest sculpture originally honored America's friendship with France, but came to symbolize freedom.

SCULPTING NATURE

Sculpting the natural elements of the world into fountains and gardens can produce spectacular results. These creations soothe and captivate us, continuing the tradition of the Hanging Gardens of Babylon, but sometimes in less traditional ways.

▼ PARADISE WITHIN

On the outside, Spain's Alhambra is a fortress. Inside, it's a paradise. Fountains, gardens, sculptures, orchards, and pools fill this palace built for Moorish kings.

TWICE CREATED

The painter Claude Monet built this picturesque water garden (in photo at top) in Giverny, France. It is an image you may very well recognize as the subject of a famous painting by the artist (bottom), called *White Waterlilies and Bridge*.

▼ PARK IT HERE

It has an Egyptian monument, a huge lake, a zoo, playgrounds, an art museum, a reservoir, and 840 acres of grounds. It once housed the biggest classical music concert ever, with 800,000 spectators. New York City's Central Park was designed over a century ago, and thousands of people count on it to this day for a nature getaway.

A-MAZE-ING

Ever get lost among 16,180 yew trees? At Longleat in Great Britain, you can. But this isn't a forest, it's a *maze* with the longest path length in the world—1.69 miles.

COOL POOL

In the city, a fountain is a cool relief from the buildings and streets. In Rome, Trevi Fountain attracts a number of admirers. According to local belief, a coin tossed in the fountain promises the visitor a return to Rome.

WATERWORKS ▶

At King Louis's Versailles, there are acres of sculpted ground and some pretty spectacular fountains. This one is full of frogs and lizards. Based on a Roman myth, the fountain tells the story of Latona, a goddess insulted by peasants. As punishment, the almighty god, Jupiter, turned the peasants into frogs and lizards.

TOWER POWER

In the early days, when you wanted a view of the city, you would climb a tower—the castle's tower, or perhaps the church's tower. During the early 20th century, as technology improved, towers took on new power and began scraping the sky.

▲ PILE OF TILE

From 1921 to 1954, working alone in Watts, near Los Angeles, Simon Rodia turned cement, steel rods, tiles, shells, and broken glass into towers up to 100 feet high. Then he left town, but his Watts Towers remain, even surviving earthquakes.

◄ FINE DINING

More than 1,800 feet high, Toronto's Canadian National Tower is the tallest structure today. Built between 1973 and 1975, and costing about $60 million, the broadcasting tower can withstand winds of 260 miles per hour. From a restaurant near the summit, diners can see up to 75 miles.

THE GREAT EMPIRE

For many people, the greatest tower is New York's Empire State Building. More than 1,000 feet tall, weighing more than 350,000 tons, and built by more than 3,000 workers in record time (less than 18 months), the Empire State was the tallest building from 1931 to 1972.

A MEAN LEAN ▶

One of the world's most famous towers is one of its shortest—the 179-foot Leaning Tower of Pisa in Italy. Built as a church tower in 1173, it began to teeter while still under construction. The marble monolith leans more than 12 feet, because the soil beneath it is soft, and the foundation is not deep enough.

◀ **HIGH LIGHT**

In Japan stands the world's tallest lighthouse. Yokohama's 348-foot Marine Tower rises nearly as high as the lighthouse of Alexandria did. People 20 miles away can see its light. But Marine Tower is more than a tall lamp. It has a restaurant, museum, aviary, and observation platform.

NEW TOWER ▶

At 1,476 feet, the Petronas Twin Towers in Kuala Lumpur, Malaysia, rival Chicago's Sears Tower. Designed by Cesar Pelli, the towers have a high-strength concrete frame and walls of stainless steel.

TWIN TRADES ▶

Though not the tallest, New York's World Trade Center is the *largest* office building, with about 9 million square feet of floor space. The center's twin towers, built between 1966 and 1973, rise about 1,300 feet and were for a short time the world's tallest buildings.

▼ BRACE AGAINST THE WIND

Nearly 1,500 feet high (plus about 200 feet of TV antenna), Chicago's Sears Tower became the tallest office building when it opened in the mid-1970s. The skyscraper is actually several towers that brace each other against falling.

LET'S GET GOING

Most people don't think of getting from place to place as miraculous. Yet, travel that once took days to accomplish is now measured in hours. Transportation, which is faster and easier than ever before, has inspired some of the most awesome structures on Earth.

▲ FALLING DOWN?

London Bridge is falling down? The song is a little old. The bridge that now stands in London is fairly sturdy (above). But an earlier bridge was in pretty bad shape at one time. Purchased by the state of Arizona, it now stands in Lake Havasu City, spanning the lake created by Parker Dam and surrounded by an English-style village.

▲ IT'S SOME REACH!

A suspension bridge is a roadway held up by wires that pass over towers and are securely fastened at both ends. New York's 4,260-foot Verrazano-Narrows Bridge is so long that it curves as the Earth does. Its wires could reach halfway to the moon.

GOLDEN GATE BRIDGE

It's not really made of gold, but it is greatly treasured. This bridge spans the entrance to San Francisco Bay, the strait that was named Golden Gate in 1846 by explorer John Charles Frémont. The rust-colored steel towers, which are the tallest in the world, give this suspension bridge a beauty recognized the world over.

▲ PLOWING PANAMA

Until 1914, going from the Atlantic to the Pacific meant sailing 7,000 miles around South America. Then more than 40,000 workers dug up more than 200 million cubic yards of dirt, creating a ditch over 50 miles long. Today, as many as 15,000 ships use the Panama Canal each year.

CHUNNEL ▶

Until 1994, a channel of water made it impossible to drive from Britain to France. The English Channel Tunnel, which runs more than 30 miles, is the world's longest underwater tunnel. Often called the "Chunnel," it carries the widest trains ever built and is one of the newest world wonders.

▼ SUPER HIGHWAY

What's over 15,000 miles long and runs from Alaska to Brazil? The Pan-American Highway. The world's longest road crosses Chile, Peru, Panama, Mexico, the United States, Canada, and other nations.

▼ IN SUSPENSION

When the Brooklyn Bridge opened for use in 1883, it was the longest suspension bridge world wide, connecting Brooklyn to the island of Manhattan. Started in 1869, its construction literally held commuters in suspense. At last, another way to get to work besides the ferry!

◀ CLOSING THE GAP

Don't mistake this engi-neering feat for some fantas-ic walkway. It's the Hoover Dam, built in the early 1930s on the Colorado River near Las Vegas, Nevada. Why, you might ask, would you want to stop the flow of a river? The dam harnesses water power and transforms it into electricity for the sur-ounding area.

MONUMENTAL MONUMENTS

Throughout history, certain people have inspired us so much that we feel bound to honor them through eternity. The monuments we create ensure that our heroes and heroines are remembered.

ALL IN ONE
Built between 1563 and 1584, the Escorial holds Spain's royal graves—plus a garden, library, church, college, palace, and offices. With thousands of rooms, it is one of the biggest low-lying buildings.

▲ A TOMB WITH ROOM
Indian emperor Shah Jahan built the Taj Mahal as his wife's tomb. Its outer walls are covered in white marble, and the interior is inlaid with jade, crystal, and other treasures. Outside, there are gardens and canals. The Taj Mahal took about 20 years to build.

▲ ON GUARD
Near Egypt's pyramids stands the Sphinx. Built more than 4,000 years ago, the rock sculpture has a man's face on a lion's body. At around 200 feet long and 66 feet high, the Sphinx looks powerful enough to do the job it was built to do—guard the pyramids and the people buried in them.

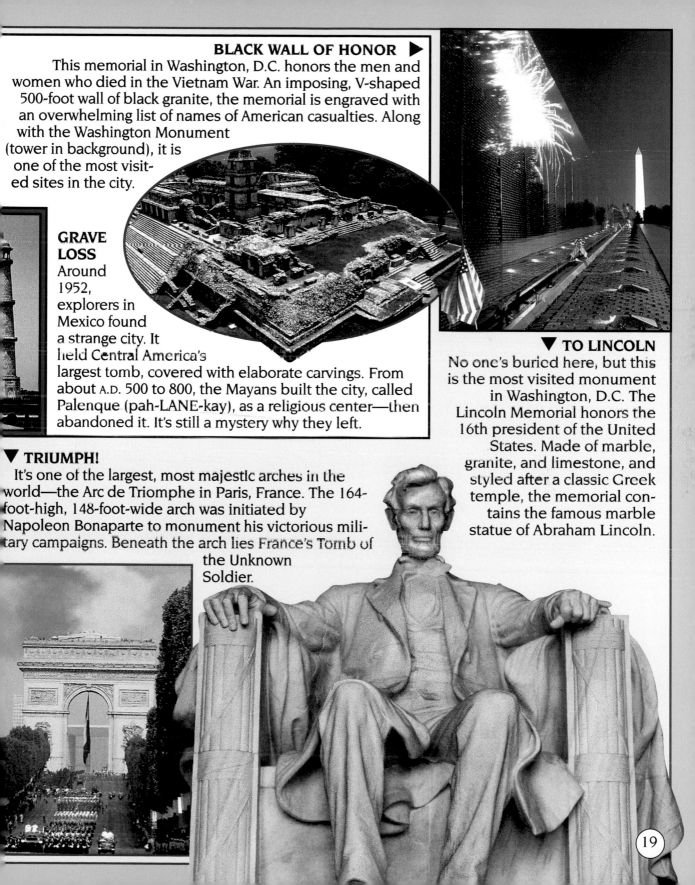

BLACK WALL OF HONOR ▶

This memorial in Washington, D.C. honors the men and women who died in the Vietnam War. An imposing, V-shaped 500-foot wall of black granite, the memorial is engraved with an overwhelming list of names of American casualties. Along with the Washington Monument (tower in background), it is one of the most visited sites in the city.

GRAVE LOSS

Around 1952, explorers in Mexico found a strange city. It held Central America's largest tomb, covered with elaborate carvings. From about A.D. 500 to 800, the Mayans built the city, called Palenque (pah-LANE-kay), as a religious center—then abandoned it. It's still a mystery why they left.

▼ TRIUMPH!

It's one of the largest, most majestic arches in the world—the Arc de Triomphe in Paris, France. The 164-foot-high, 148-foot-wide arch was initiated by Napoleon Bonaparte to monument his victorious military campaigns. Beneath the arch lies France's Tomb of the Unknown Soldier.

▼ TO LINCOLN

No one's buried here, but this is the most visited monument in Washington, D.C. The Lincoln Memorial honors the 16th president of the United States. Made of marble, granite, and limestone, and styled after a classic Greek temple, the memorial contains the famous marble statue of Abraham Lincoln.

CITYSCAPE

One of the most breathtaking sights is a cityscape—its skyscrapers, domed buildings, spires, bridges, and lights. Historically, cities grew out of people's need to protect themselves. So dwellings were built within a walled area, usually along a river. In modern times, cities have become the places where most people live and work. Some are real wonders.

SKYSCRAPER ISLAND

One of the world's leading commercial, financial, and cultural centers, New York is the most populated city in the United States. Today the Manhattan skyline is dominated by skyscrapers. But when it was first colonized in the early 17th century by the Dutch, Manhattan was a green island inhabited by Native Americans.

WORLD LINK ▲

Situated on both sides of the Bosporus, the strait that separates Europe and Asia, the city of Istanbul links the East to the West. This very old city was founded by Roman Emperor Constantine I in A.D. 324, and until 1930 was known as Constantinople.

LONDON TOWN ▼

Occupied by Rome in the first century A.D., London, England, has been beset by war, epidemics, and other crises. The city was heavily bombed by German airplanes and zeppelins during World War II, and reconstruction really altered the face of the skyline. Many landmarks still remain, however. One London favorite is the bell known as Big Ben, which is part of the Clock Tower at the Houses of Parliament.

VILLAGE ▶ TO CAPITAL

Copenhagen was at one time a simple fishing village, but it became increasingly influential as a port city. Today it remains the capital city of Denmark.

◀ ABBEY ISLAND

Is this rocky, cone-shaped islet a city? As you approach Mont-Saint-Michel in northwestern France, it may seem more like a vision, especially at high tide when surrounded by water. In fact, the settlement is celebrated for its Benedictine abbey, the church of which stands 240 feet above sea level.

▼CHANGING HANDS

Once a haven for pirates, the province of Hong Kong has transformed itself into one of the wealthiest places in the Far East. Its capital city is Victoria. The province has been a British dependency for over a century but will soon be released to China.

︰ITY OF CANALS ▲

Situated on 120 islands formed by 177 canals, he city of Venice, Italy, is connected by about 00 bridges. But the easiest and fastest way to et around is not by foot—it's by boat.

21

HOUSES OF THE HOLY

Few buildings inspire as much awe as those created for worship. Over the centuries, religion has been of central importance in people's lives, and enormous funds have gone into building magnificent churches, temples, and mosques for worshipers.

MARBLE ▲ MARVEL

Ornately decorated in red, green, and white marble, the red-domed Cathedral of Santa Maria del Fiore dominates the city of Florence. Companions to the cathedral are the bell tower and baptistery. The baptistery is famous for its gilded bronze doors depicting scenes from the Old Testament.

▲ MASTERPIECE

The Sistine Chapel is perhaps best known for its ceiling. For four years, Michelangelo and his assistants painted 10,000 square feet, illustrating 300 Biblical figures and the universe's creation—even though as a sculptor he disliked painting and didn't want the job.

HOUSE OF THE HOLY

The chief synagogue of Jesus' time is now called the Dome of the Rock mosque. By any name, this building in Jerusalem is among the world's holiest spots. Moslems say that Mohammed rose to heaven here, the tablets of the Ten Commandments are said to be here, and Jews still pray at the temple's Wailing Wall.

CRYSTAL CHURCH ▶

The Crystal Cathedral in Garden Grove, California, is shaped like a four-pointed sparkling star. The more than 10,000 panes of glass cover a weblike steel structure to form translucent walls. The church also has a large screen outside to allow drive-in worshipers to pray on their way.

▼ BASIL BEAUTY

In the midst of Russia's austere Kremlin stands the extravagant St. Basil's Cathedral. Constructed by Czar Ivan the Terrible, its onion-shaped, vividly colored domes are world famous. Legend has it that Ivan blinded the architect so that he could never create anything so beautiful again.

◀ DROPPING ANGKOR

The biggest religious structure of all, Angkor Wat temple in Cambodia, took almost 40 years to build. It covers nearly a square mile, has a wide moat, chiseled walls, and a main temple over 200 feet tall.

▼ BUDDHA'S BEST

No Thai shrine is more revered than the Temple of the Emerald Buddha. Of all its treasures, the greatest is the smallest—a jade statue of Buddha less than 3 feet high, placed on a huge gold altar.

HOUSE FOR A GODDESS

Built as a temple to the goddess Athena, Greece's Parthenon once housed statues and other treasures. It's now empty, yet is still revered as one of the world's most perfect structures.

SHOWING OFF

In the Middle Ages, people came together at fairs to buy and sell goods, and occasionally for amusement. In modern times fairs have become international events known as expositions, showcasing advances in technology and driving forward new inventions. The quest for new thrills and entertainment has also inspired some pretty incredible amusement parks.

OLD COASTER

Amusement is the idea behind Copenhagen's Tivoli Gardens, which were opened in 1843. Besides the pavilions and open-air theaters, Tivoli has kept up with the thrills and chills of the machine age by adding an amusement park. In fact, it has the oldest operating roller coaster, constructed in 1913.

INVENTING THE WHEEL

Today's high-energy theme-park rides are driven by electricity. It was not until the exposition in Chicago in 1893 that electricity was introduced to the public. Celebrating Columbus's discovery of America, this show also presented the Ferris wheel, which became a popular ride and drove forward the creation of amusement parks.

HOT RIDES

Coney Island amusement park in Brooklyn, NY, had one of the first roller coasters. A Ferris wheel was installed as early as 1894. In the 1940s, during its heyday, the park's parachute ride was all the rage— except when people got stuck at the top.

At Haw Par Villa, a Singapore theme park, boating through a dragon provides some of the local fun.

New technology in building and engineering has been the main focus in the 20th-century world fairs. The exposition held in Montreal in 1967 had "Man and His World" as its theme. This huge sphere erected for the show still stands.

▼ WHAT A WORLD!

Disney World is the biggest privately funded building program ever, and it's the world's largest amusement park, covering 30,000 acres. The park's symbol is Spaceship Earth, a large sphere about 180 feet tall.

THE REVOLUTIONARY

Built for the 1889 exposition in honor of the French Revolution, the Eiffel Tower was itself a revolution—in engineering. Alexandre Eiffel raised the wrought-iron structure to nearly 1,000 feet, and it remained the world's tallest structure until 1930.

HOW ENTERTAINING!

Some of the grandest structures on Earth were built for pure entertainment—for concerts, plays, games, art exhibitions, and more.

▲ LINCOLN LIGHTS

In New York City, there's a complex devoted solely to the arts. This is Lincoln Center—six buildings and an outdoor bandshell designed for musical and theatrical performances. At the center is a courtyard and fountain, which glows golden when the lights go on at show time.

▼ LONG PLAY

For 2,500 years, the Greek seaport town of Epidaurus has put on plays. To this day, other theaters copy its amphitheater (literally, "a theater on both sides"). The theater is designed so perfectly that the actors don't need microphones to reach the audience, which can number 14,000.

▼ TREASURE HOUSE

Overlooking the Neva River in St. Petersburg, the Hermitage is part of what was once a Russian royal residence. Catherine the Great created the luxurious quarters to house her art collection. Now a public museum, the Hermitage is a "treasure house," with 3 million exhibits in 12 miles of gallery space.

▲ SYDNEY'S SEASHELLS

Made of steel, glass, and concrete, the Opera House in Sydney, Australia, looks like no other structure on Earth. It reminds people of seashells or a ship in full sail—fitting images for a building that stands near the shore.

▼ PARIS PALACE

One of the largest palaces in the world, covering 48 acres, the Louvre was opened as a museum to the public in 1793 during the French Revolution. Built on the site of a recently excavated 13th-century fortress, the Louvre houses many famous paintings, including Leonardo da Vinci's *Mona Lisa*.

◀ ROMAN RECREATION

The world's most famous entertainment building is Rome's Colosseum. At 513 feet wide, 620 feet across, and more than 150 feet high, with seating of about 50,000, the Colosseum is the largest monument of Imperial Rome. Opened in A.D. 80, it was still in use more than 400 years later.

During a renovation program, completed in 1989, a glass pyramid was built to serve as the main entrance to the Louvre.

STRANGE STRUCTURES

There are so many wonders in the world—so many yet to discover. Here, you'll find some wonders that are really unusual, or still unexplained, or just unbelievable oddities! You have to wonder, what else is out there?

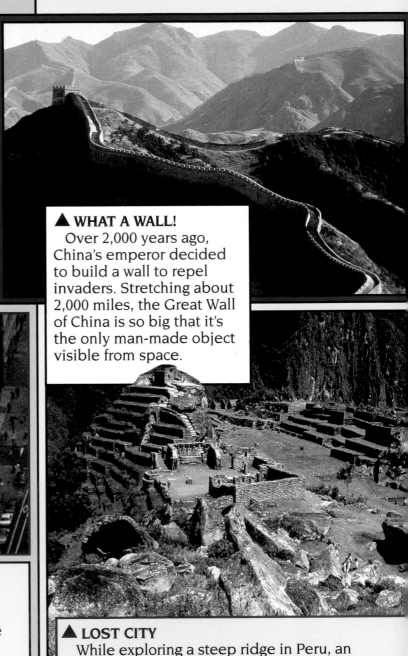

▲ WHAT A WALL!

Over 2,000 years ago, China's emperor decided to build a wall to repel invaders. Stretching about 2,000 miles, the Great Wall of China is so big that it's the only man-made object visible from space.

START SCRAPING

In 1902, folks in New York City found a prime spot for a building, except that the lot formed an angle where two avenues crossed. The solution was to build a triangular structure. This young skyscraper— the Flatiron Building—was named for its resemblance to an iron.

28

▲ LOST CITY

While exploring a steep ridge in Peru, an archaeologist stumbled on an unknown Inca city—Machu Picchu. The ancient city flourished for centuries, then was simply abandoned.

GIGANTIC GATE

Do you know what it is and why it's there? It's the world's tallest monument, and it's there to remind us that St. Louis was the pioneers' gateway to the West. At 630 feet tall and 630 feet wide, the Gateway Arch in St. Louis rises twice as high as the Statue of Liberty, stands visible from 30 miles away, and dominates every building in sight.

MYSTERY ART

On Easter Island in the South Pacific stand as many as 1,000 statues. They range roughly from 3 to 70 feet high, and weigh up to 89 tons. No one knows who made them, how they made them, why they made them, or how they moved the heavy masses of rock into the rows where they stand.

ROCK CLOCK?

Between 3,000 and 4,500 years old, England's Stonehenge is both ancient and puzzling. This strange arrangement of stones is thought to be an astrological calendar, but no one really knows for sure.

▲ CENTER OF THE EARTH

The town of Delphi was considered by the ancient Greeks to be the center of the Earth. At the temple, a priestess spoke for the god Apollo, and the oracle of Delphi was consulted by private citizens and public officials alike.

▲ SUPER SURVIVOR

The Pantheon of Rome is probably the best-preserved building of ancient Rome. Although it's now a church, it was built as a temple to all the Roman gods. A huge cylinder, this great survivor has at the center of its dome a hole, called an oculus, through which natural light enters.

29